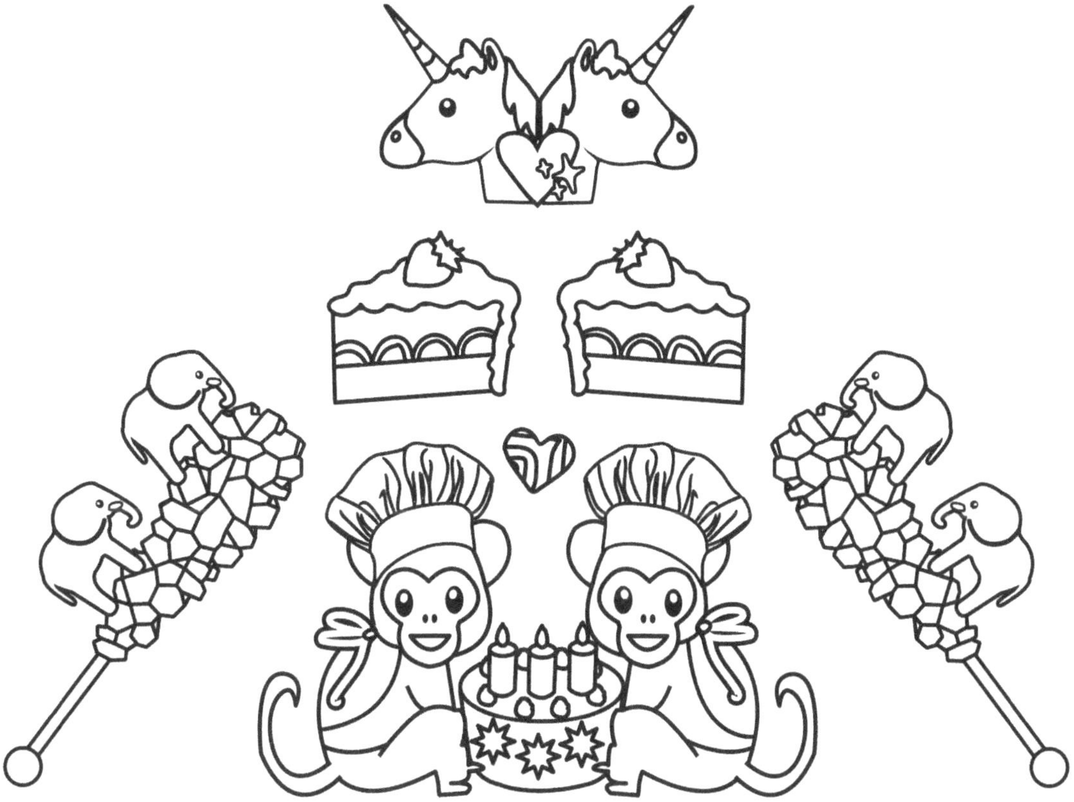

EMOJI WORLD 2

Animals, Unicorns, & Dessert OMG

24 PAGE COLORING BOOK

Illustrations by
Dani Kates

COLOR with Dani

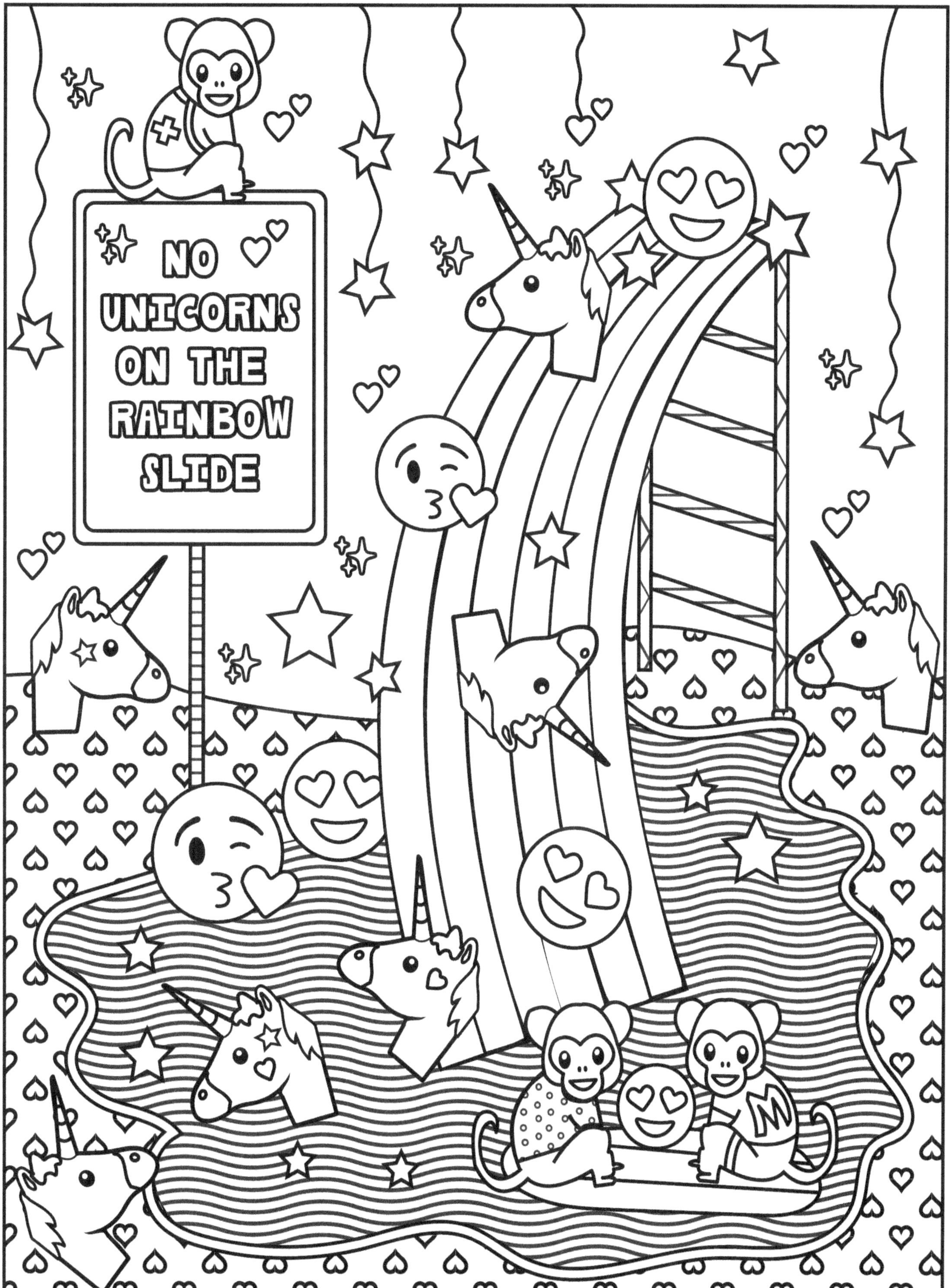
NO UNICORNS ON THE RAINBOW SLIDE

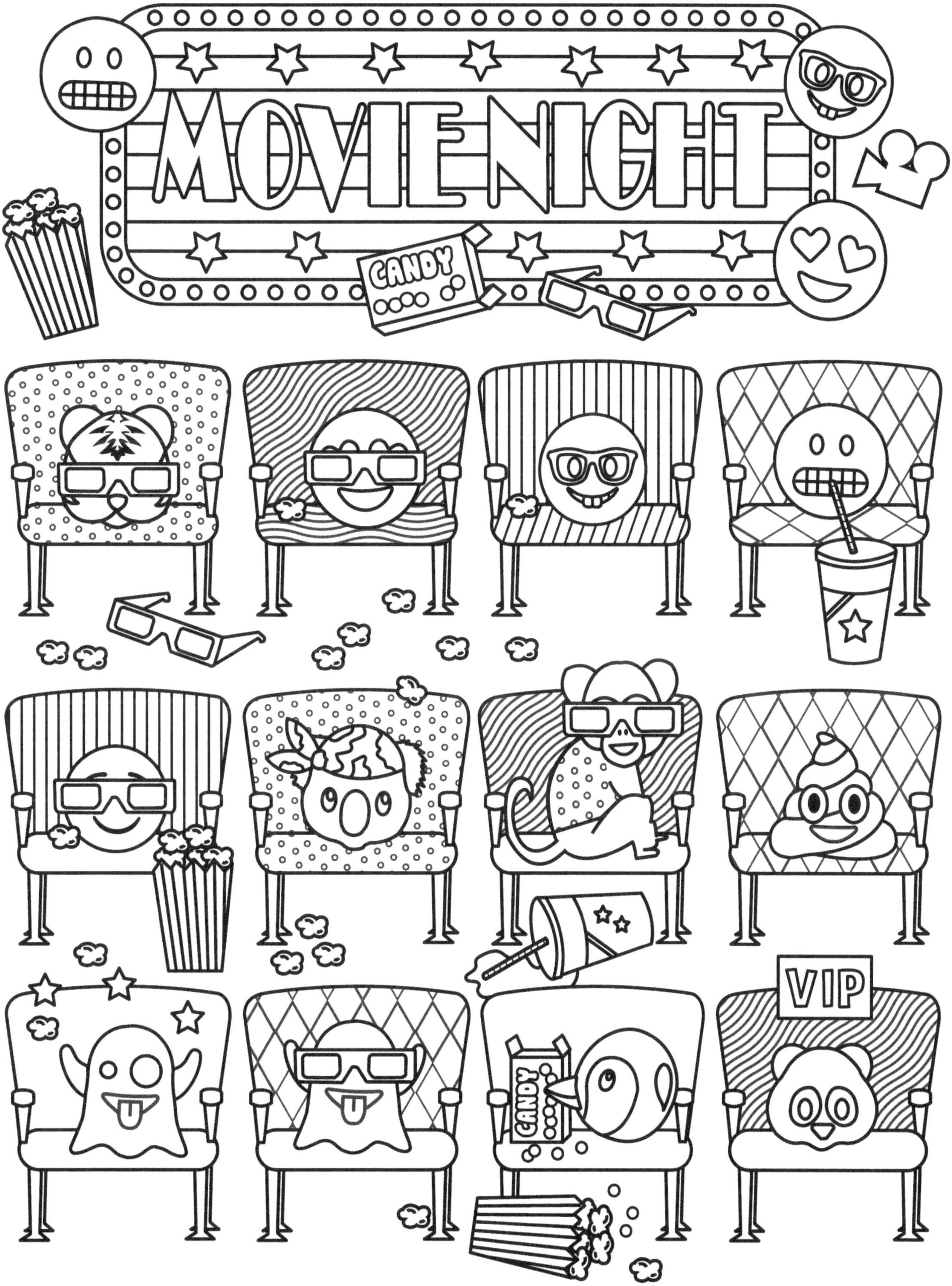
MOVIE NIGHT
CANDY
VIP
CANDY

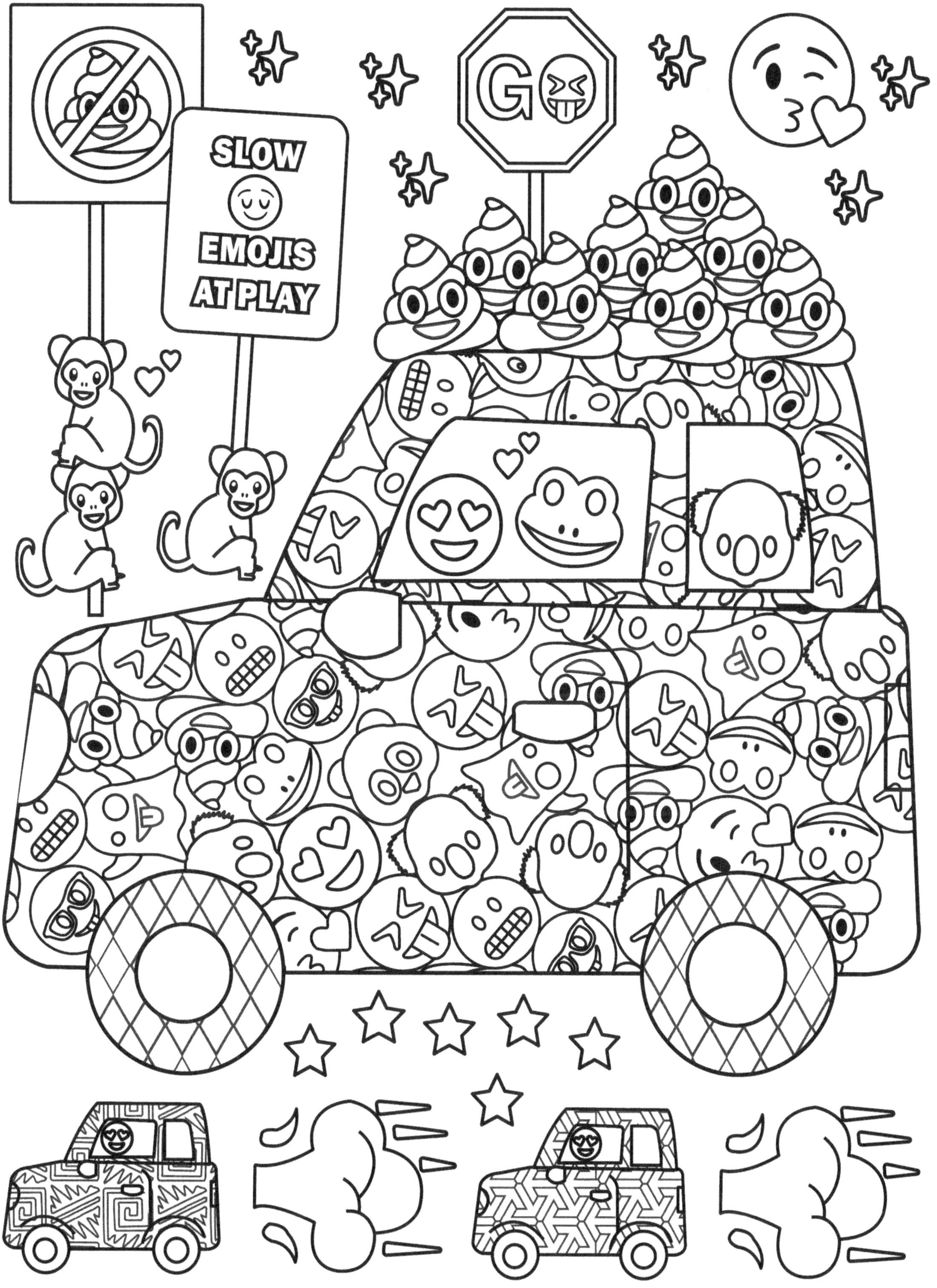
SLOW
EMOJIS
AT PLAY
GO

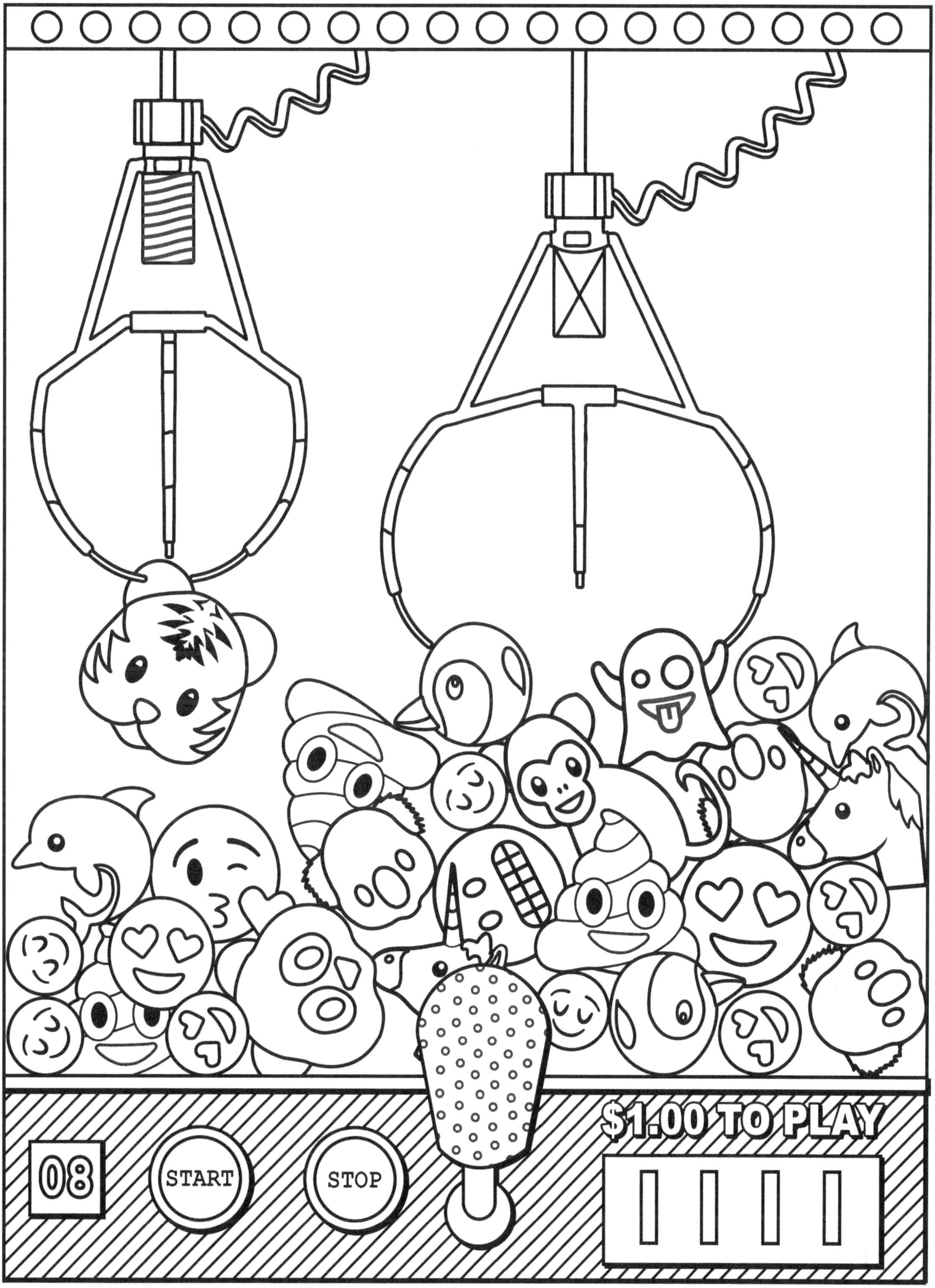

$1.00 TO PLAY
08
START
STOP

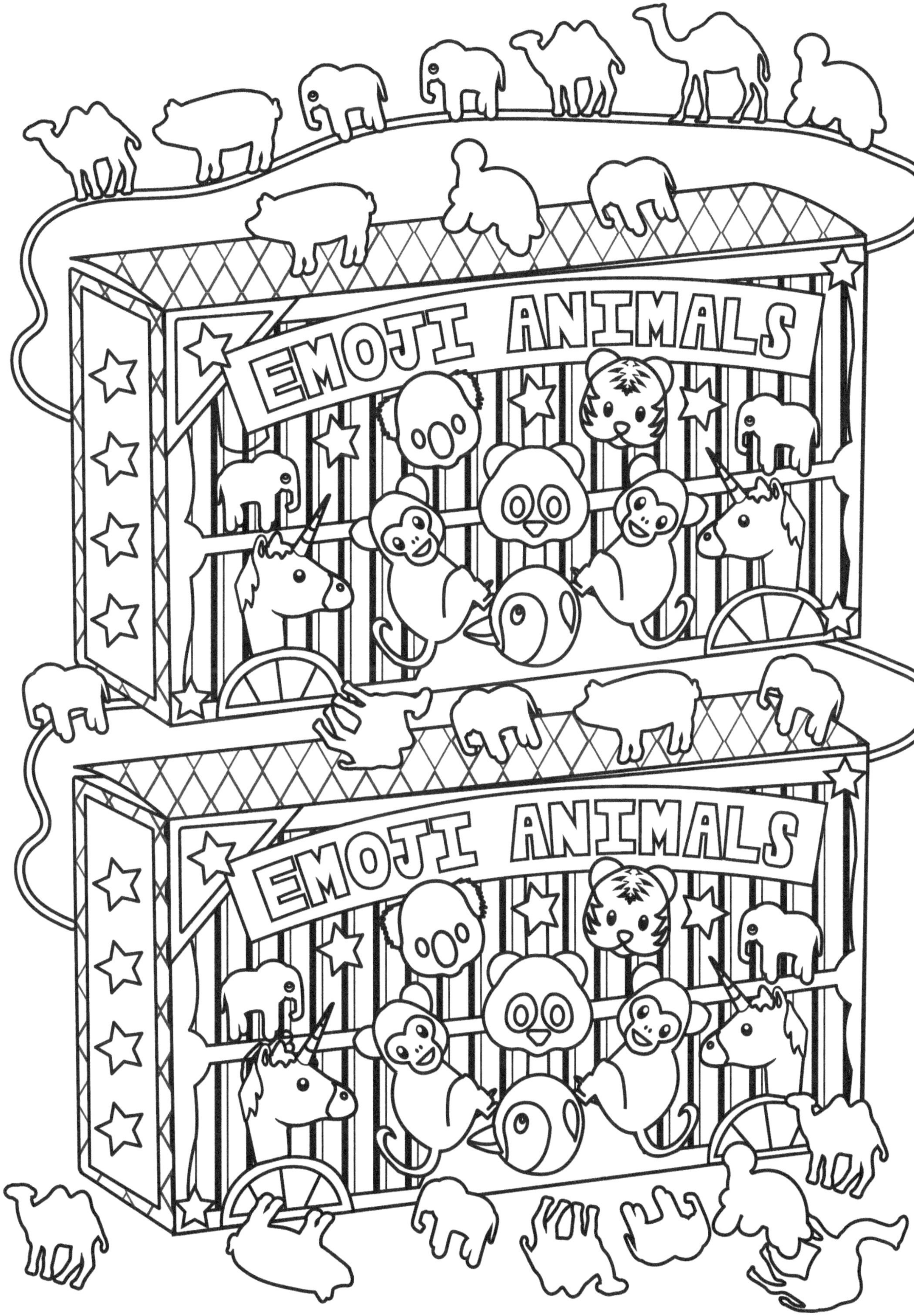
EMOJI ANIMALS
EMOJI ANIMALS

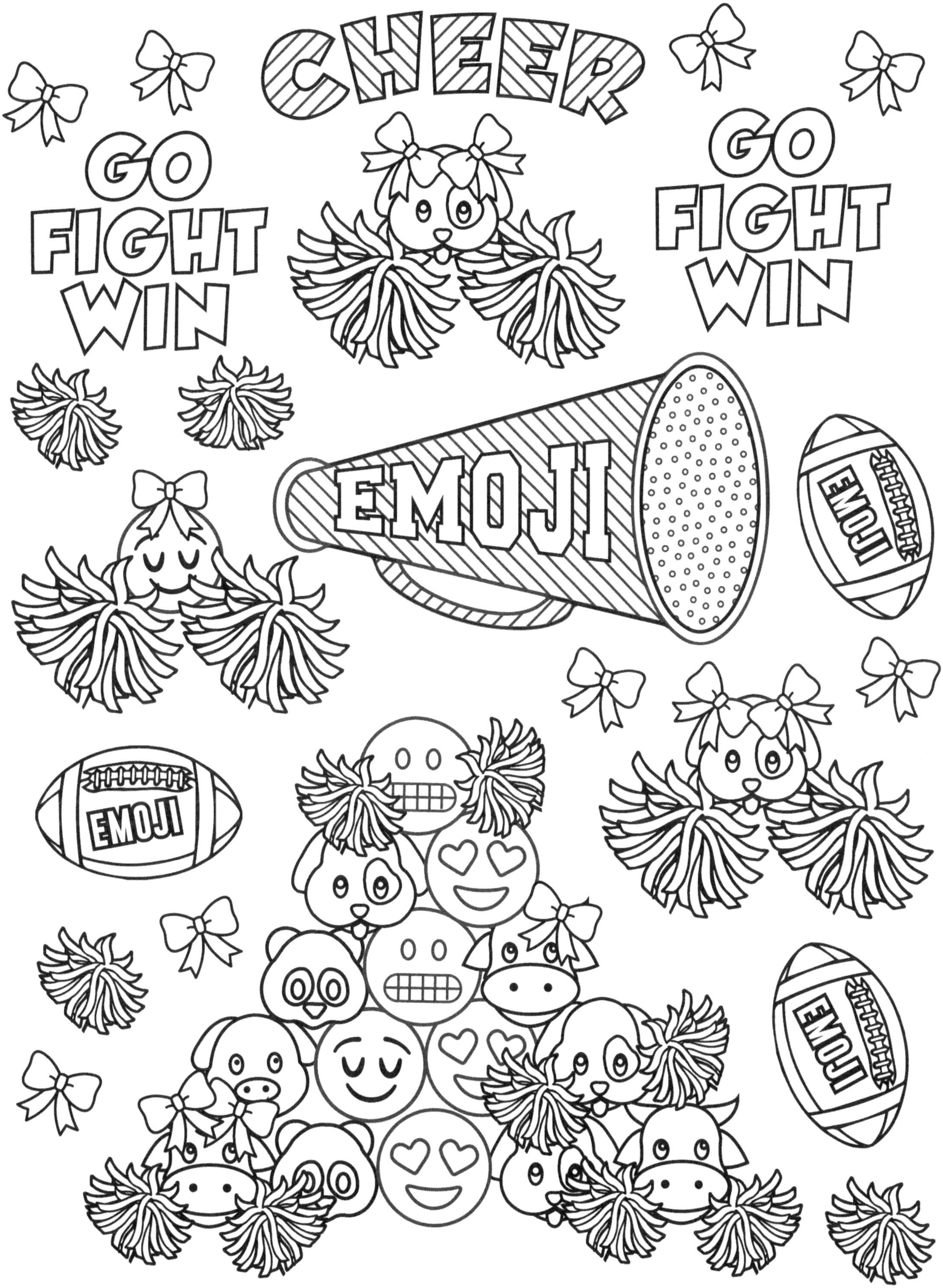
CHEER
GO FIGHT WIN
GO FIGHT WIN
EMOJI
EMOJI
EMOJI
EMOJI

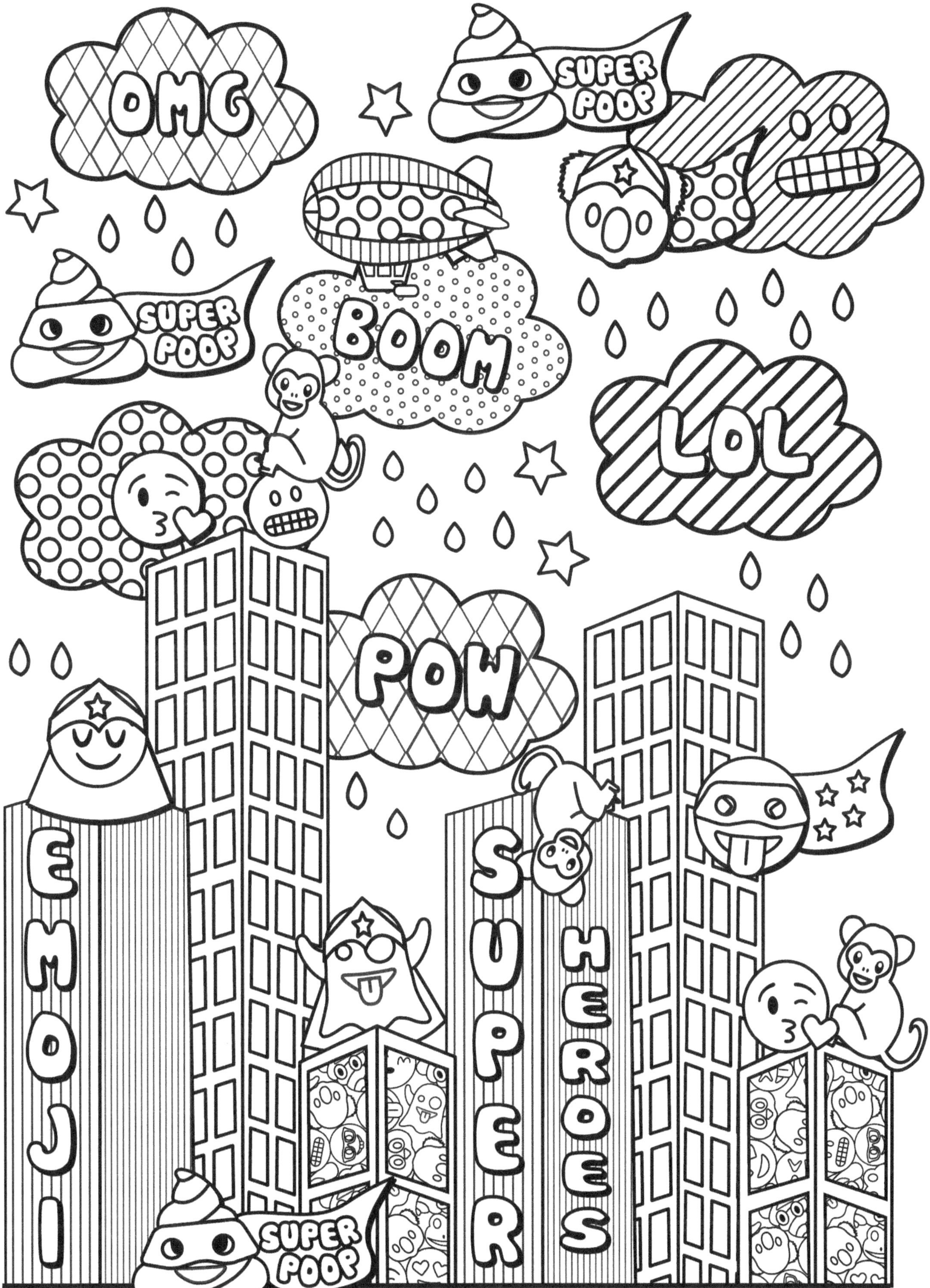
OMG
SUPER POOP
SUPER POOP
BOOM
LOL
POW
EMOJI
SUPER
HEROES
SUPER POOP

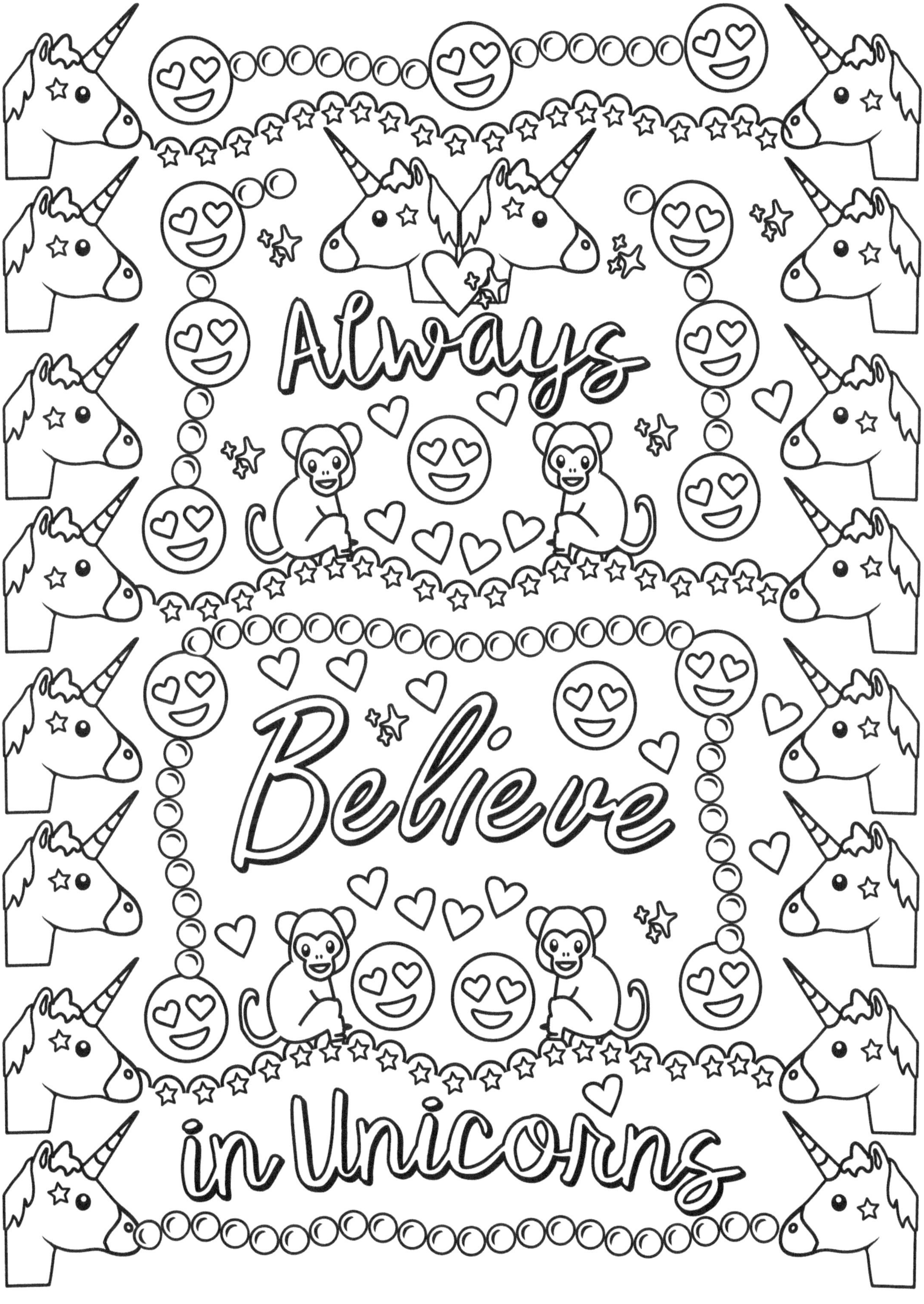
Always
Believe
in Unicorns

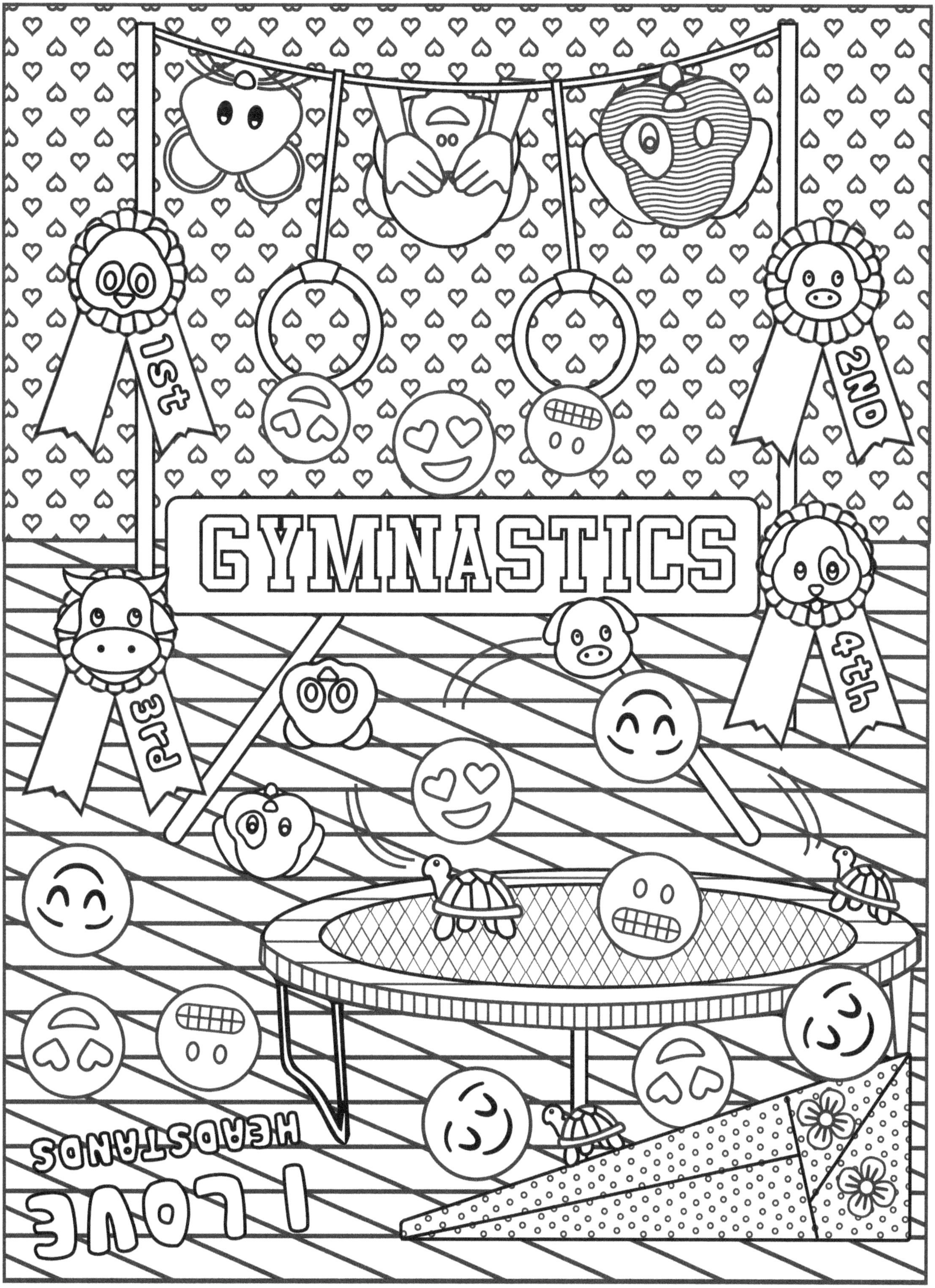
GYMNASTICS
1st
2ND
3rd
4th
I LOVE HEADSTANDS

I'M GOING ON A PICNIC AND IM BRINGING...

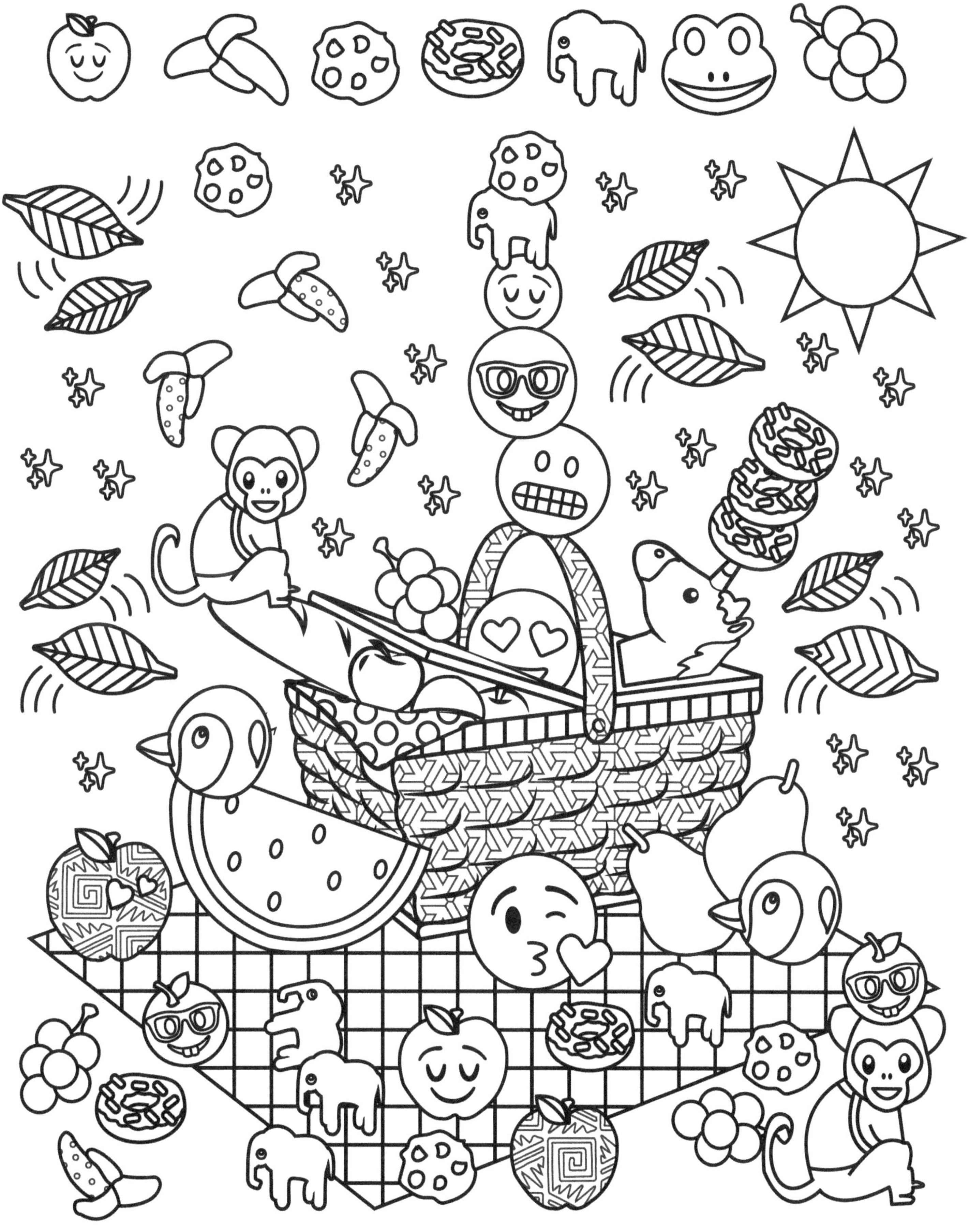

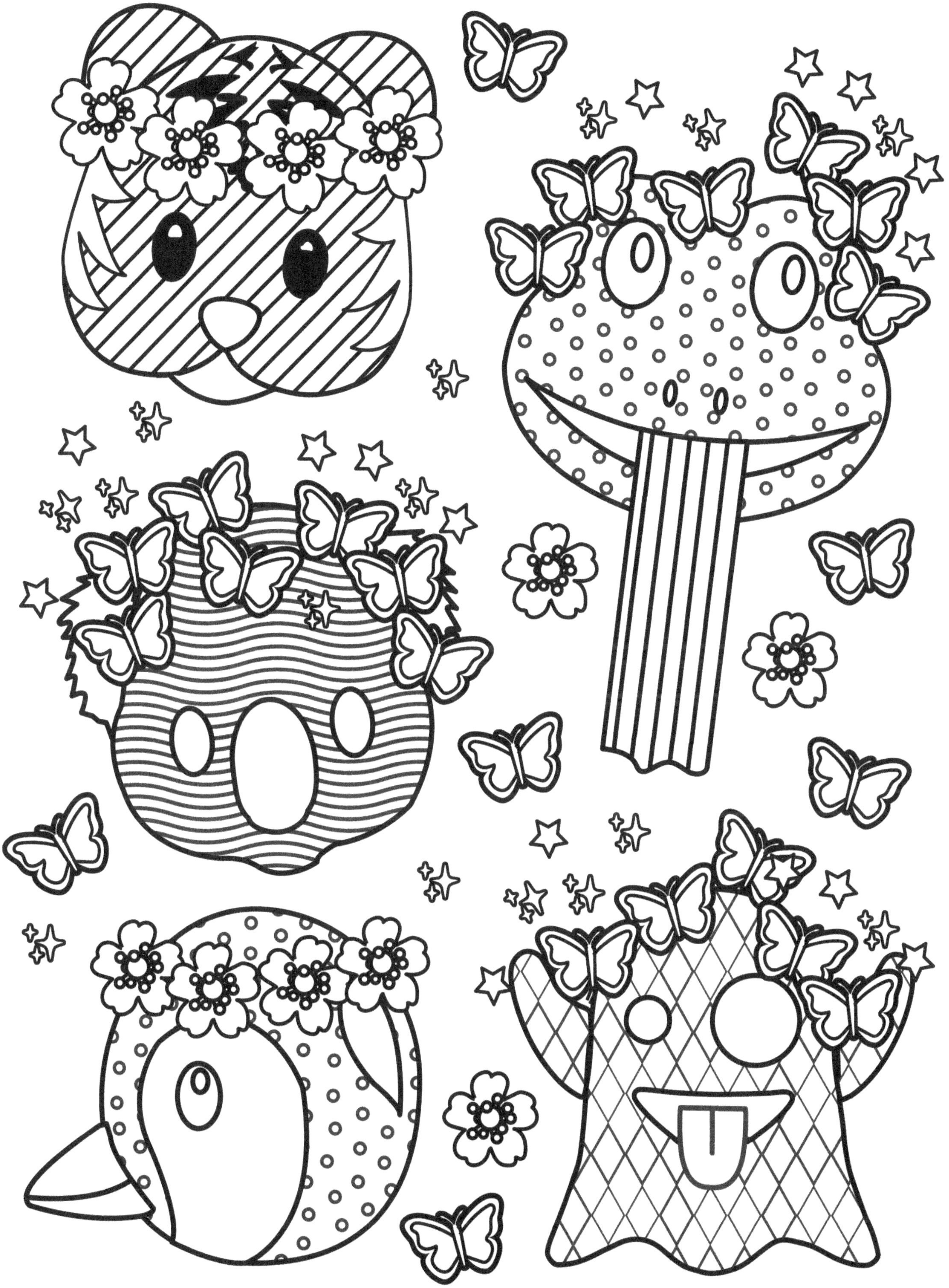

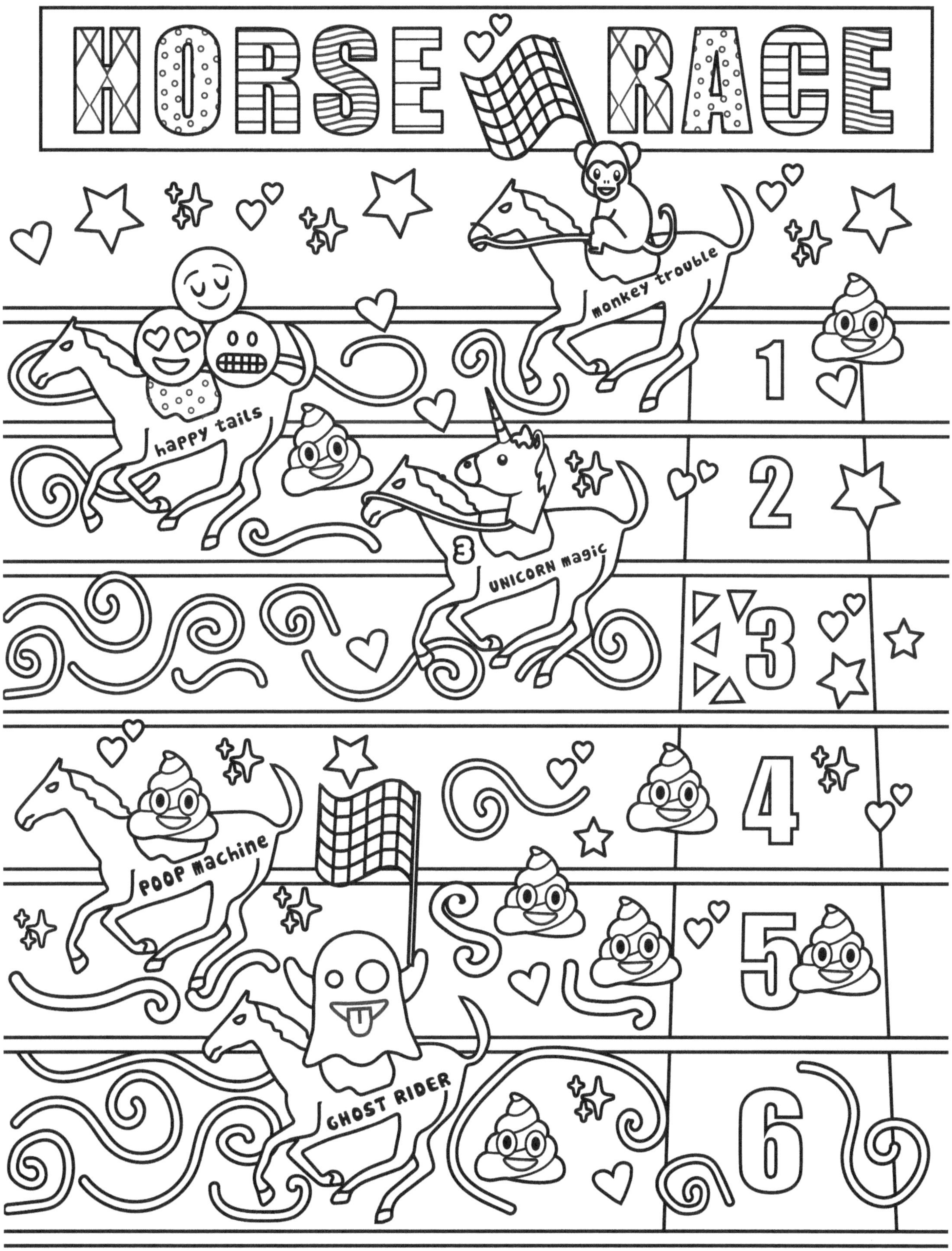
HORSE RACE
monkey trouble
happy tails
UNICORN magic
3
POOP Machine
GHOST RIDER
1
2
3
4
5
6

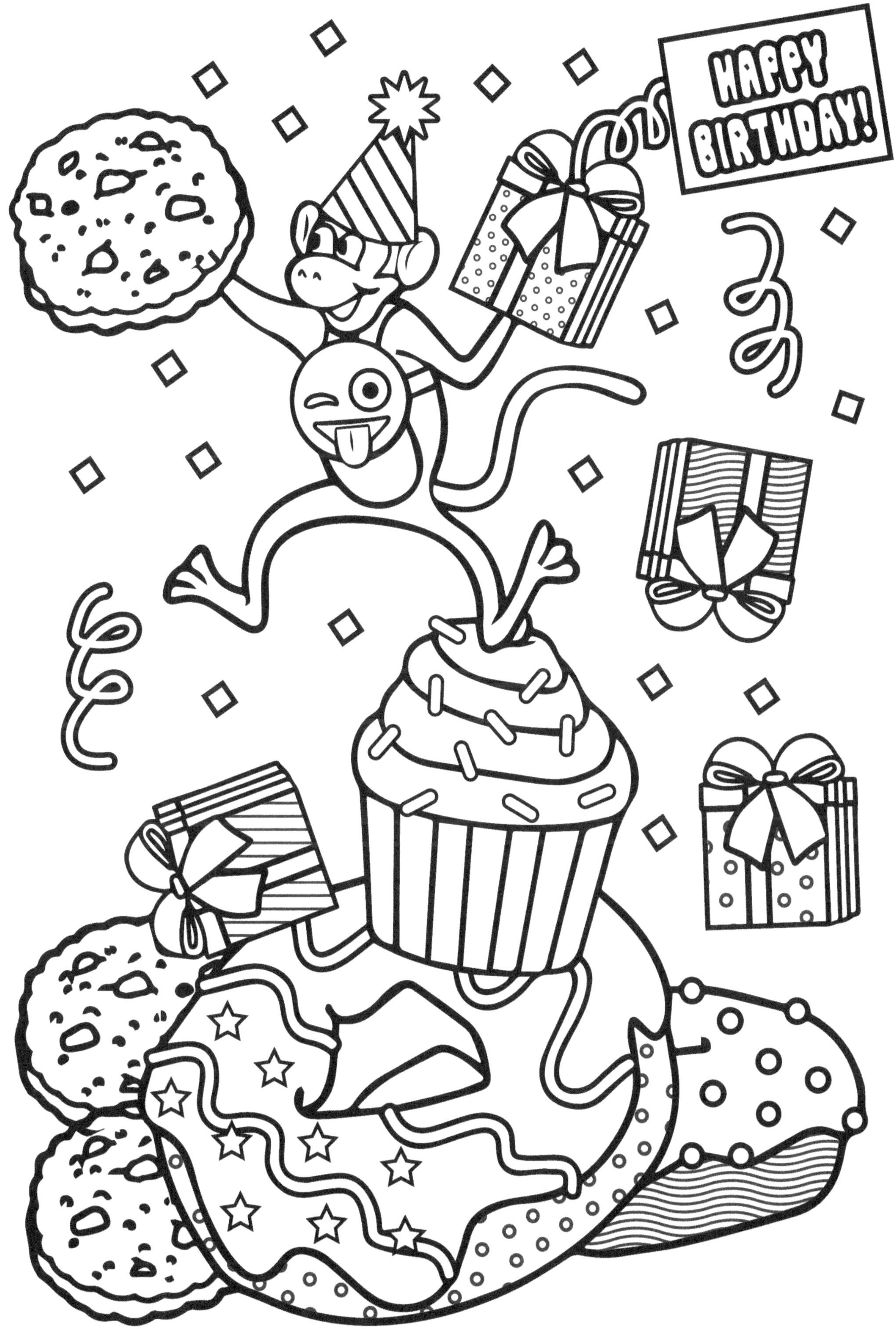
HAPPY BIRTHDAY!

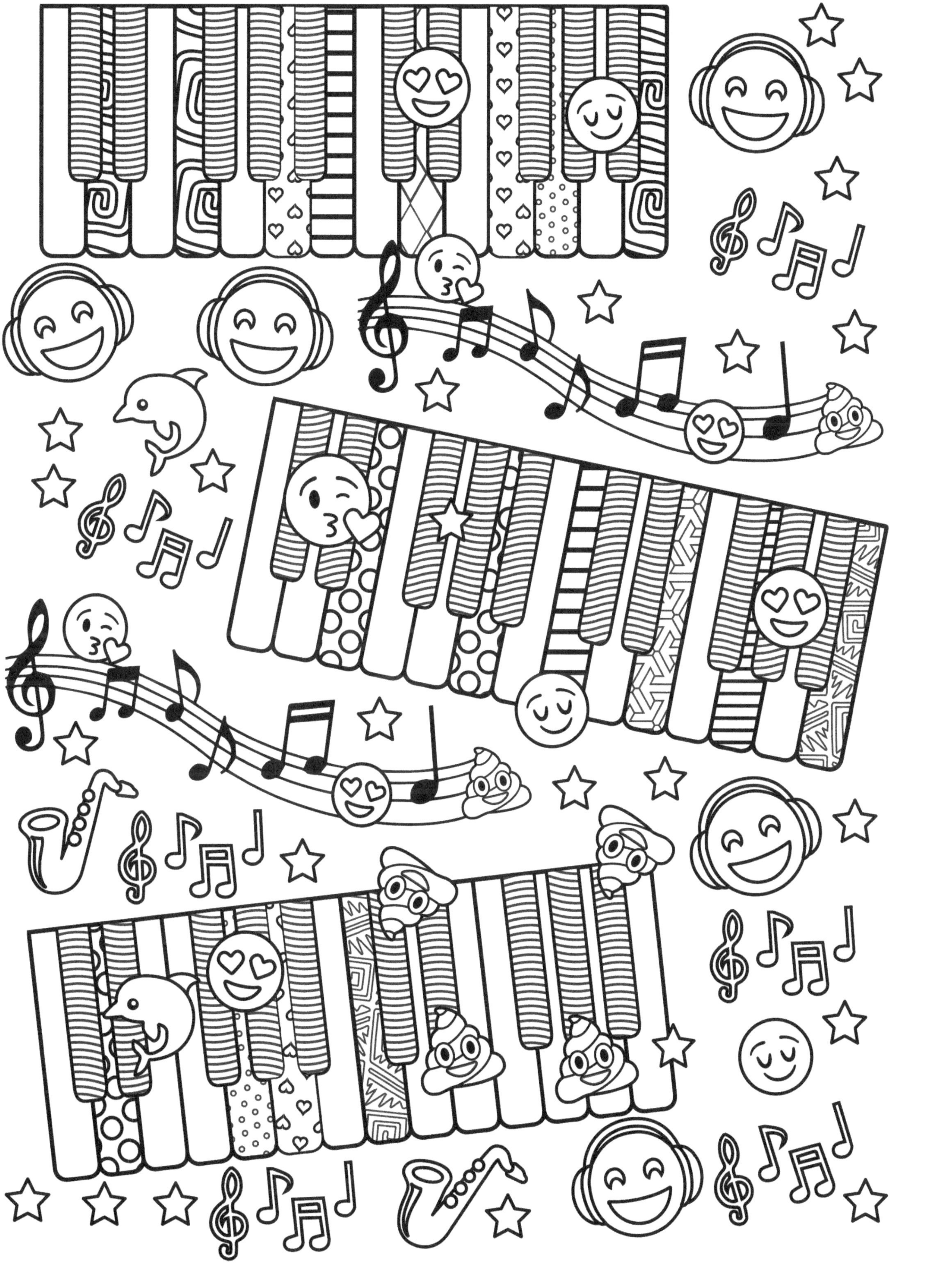

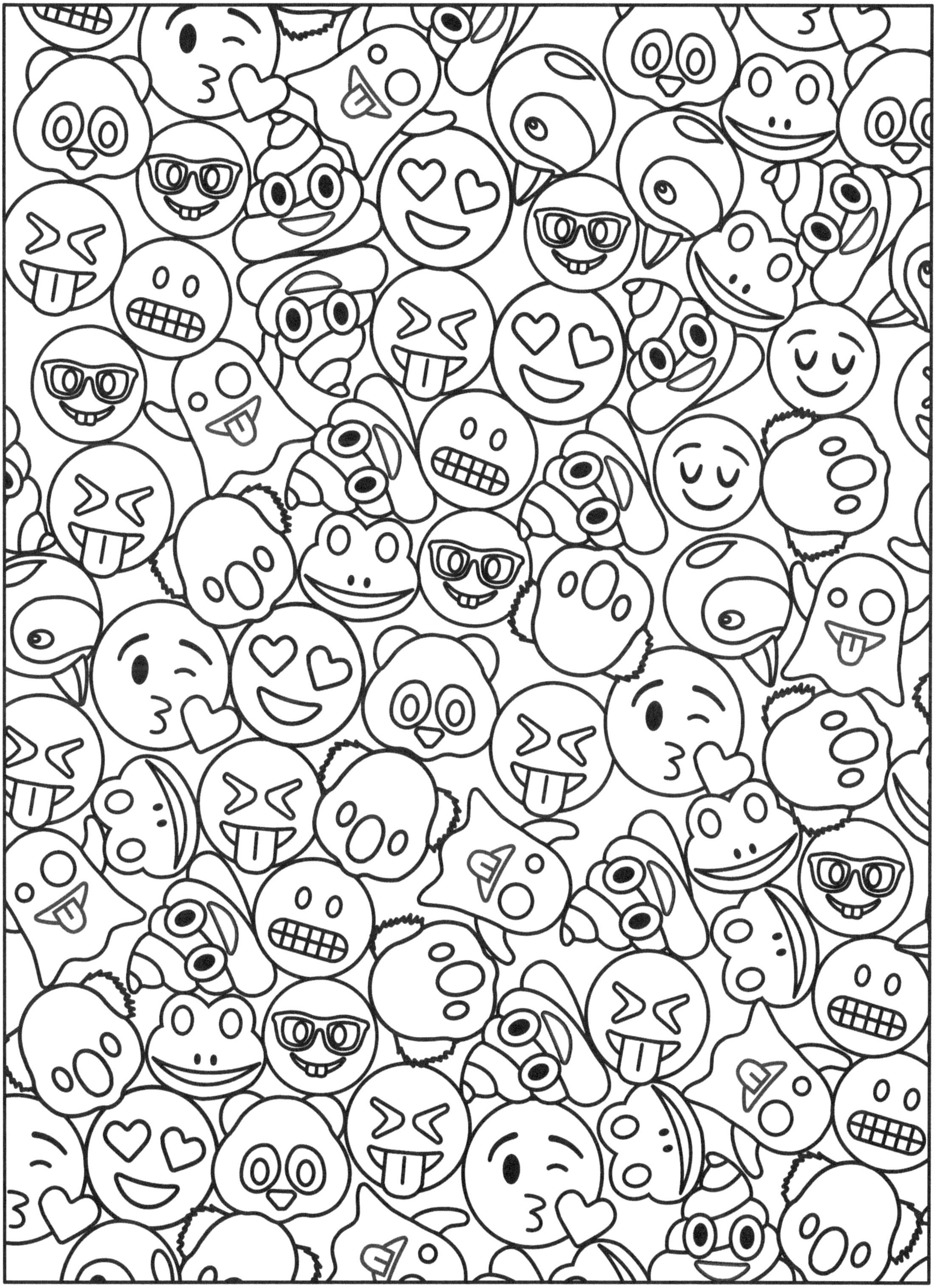

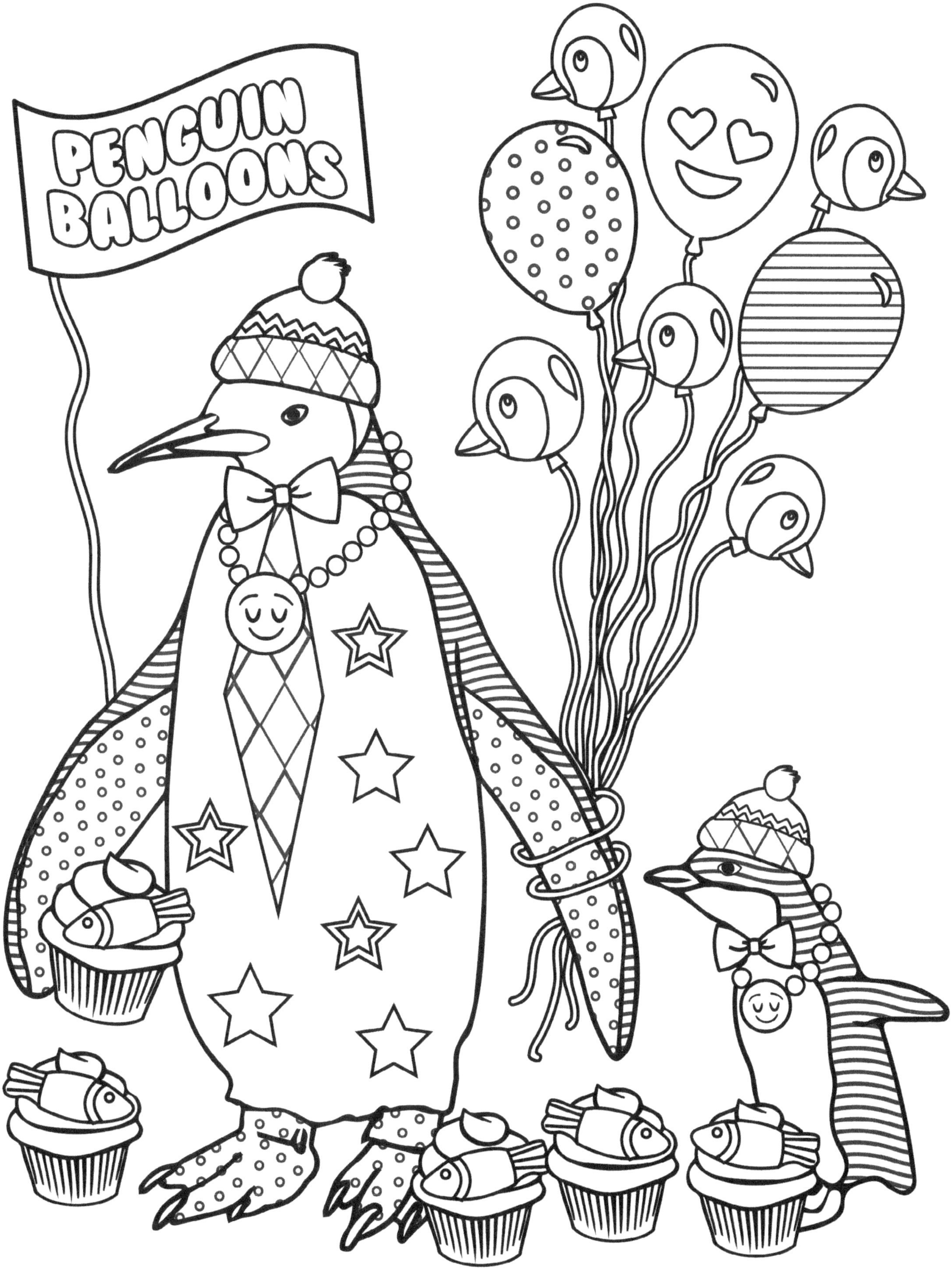
PENGUIN
BALLOONS

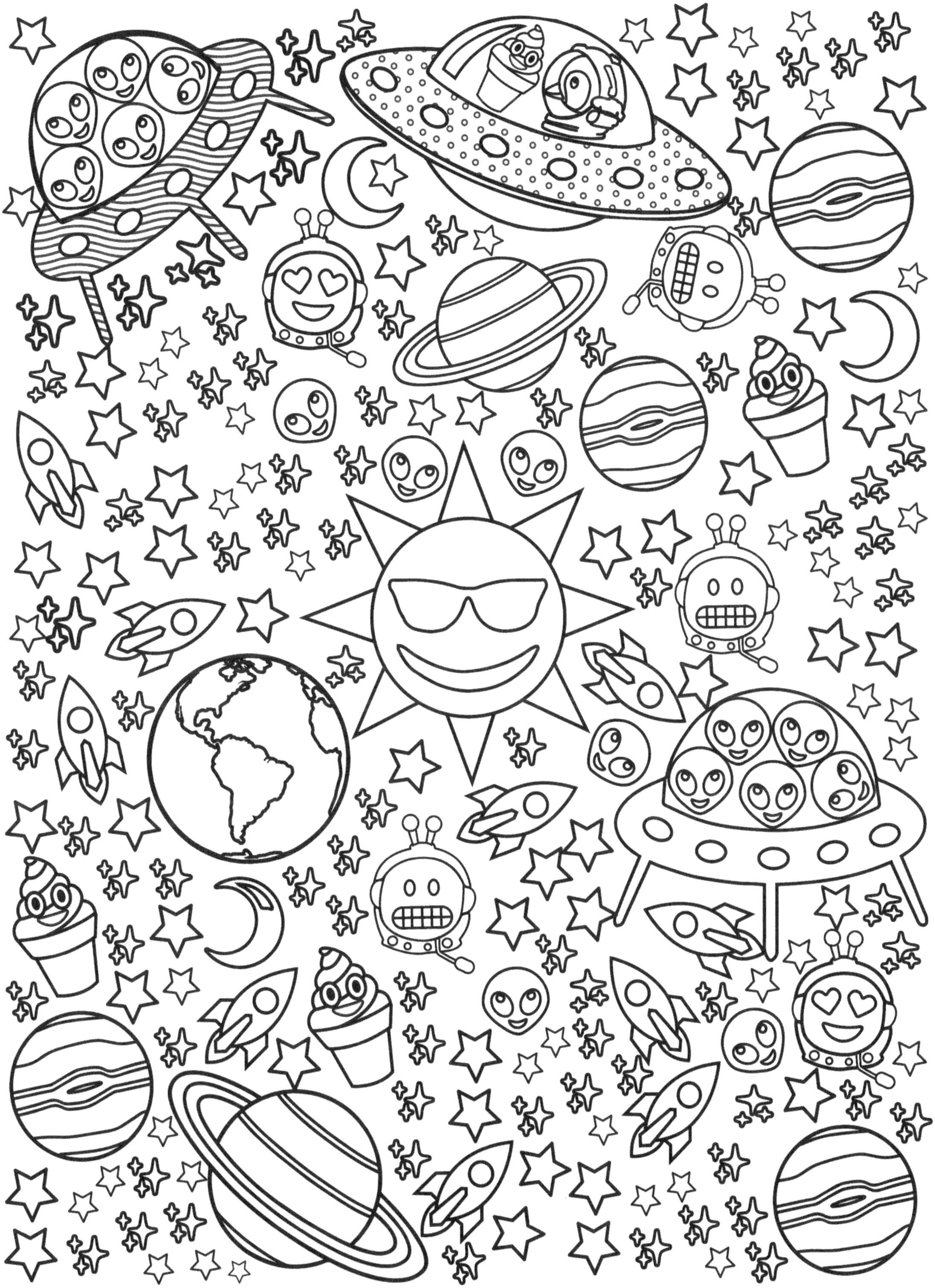

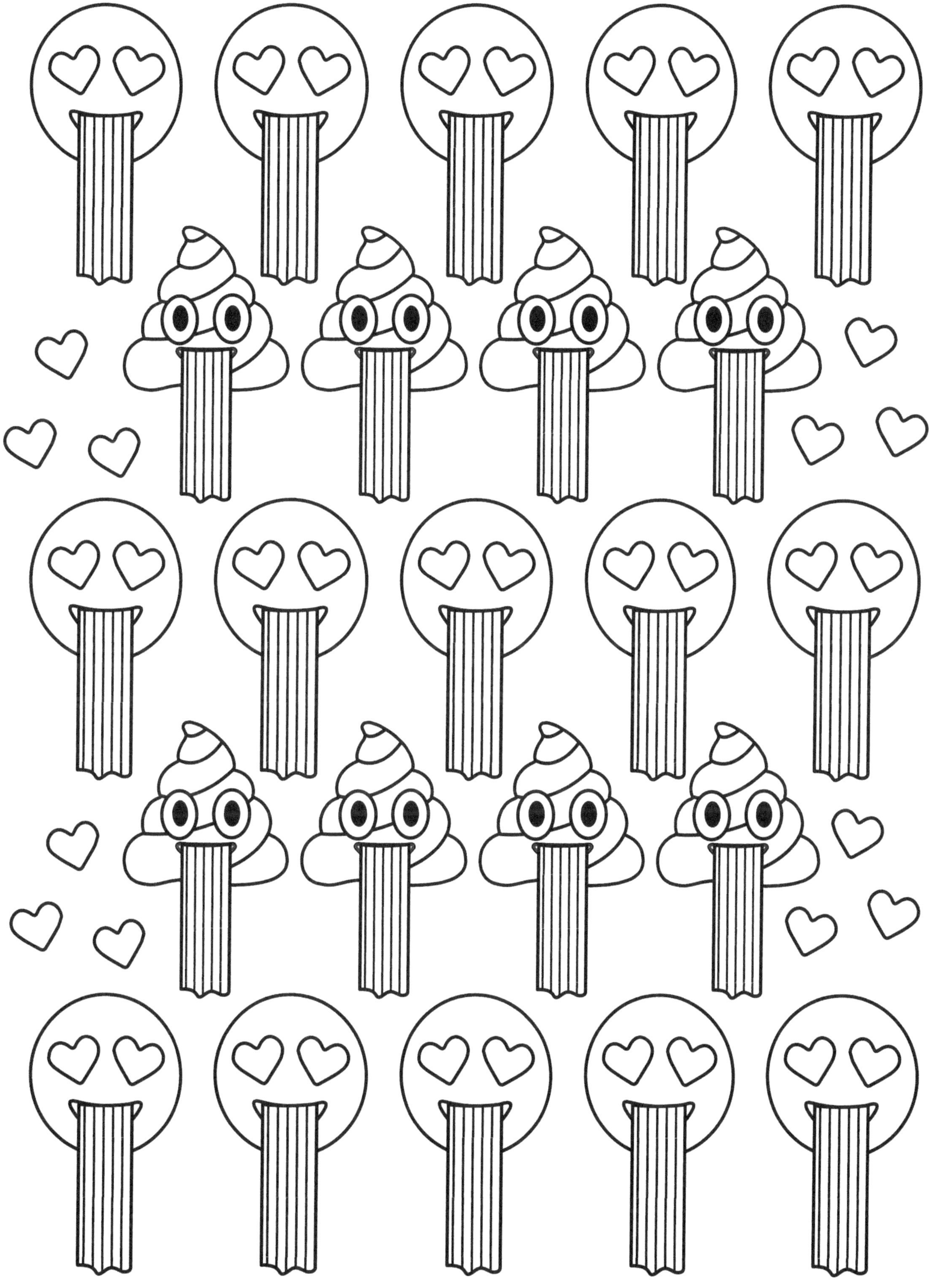

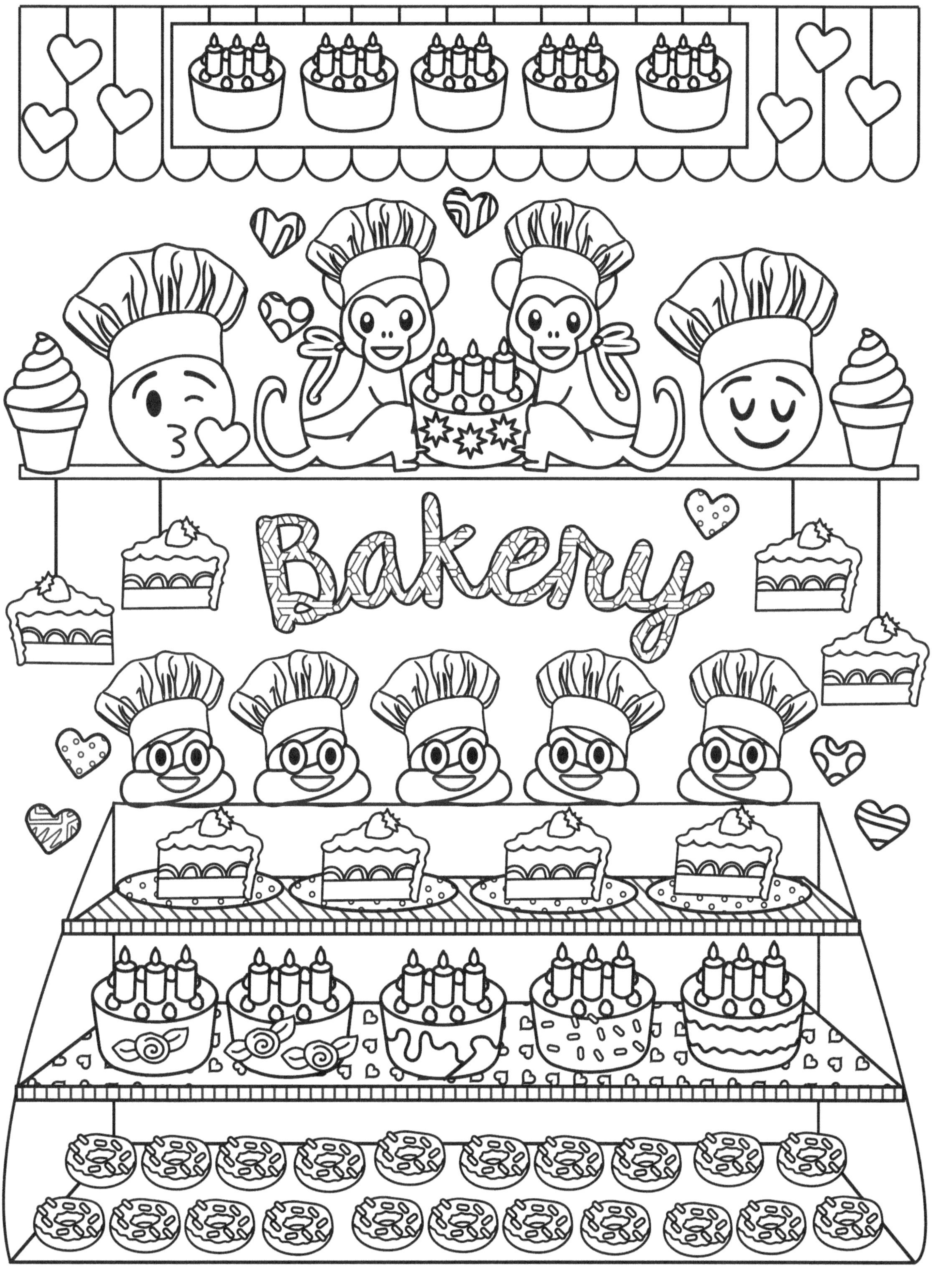
Bakery

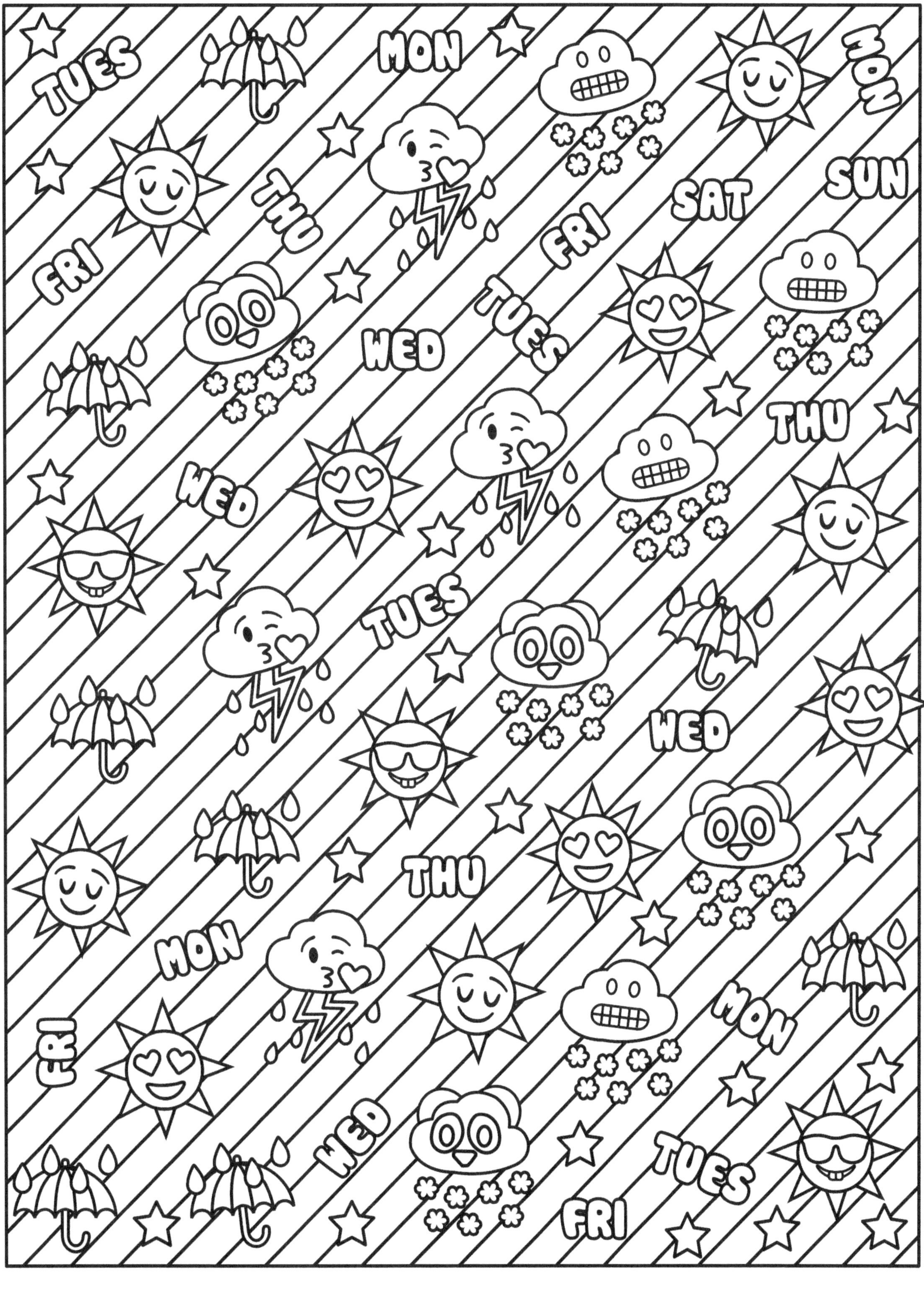
TUES
MON
MON
THU
SAT
SUN
FRI
FRI
TUES
WED
THU
WED
TUES
WED
THU
MON
MON
FRI
WED
TUES
FRI

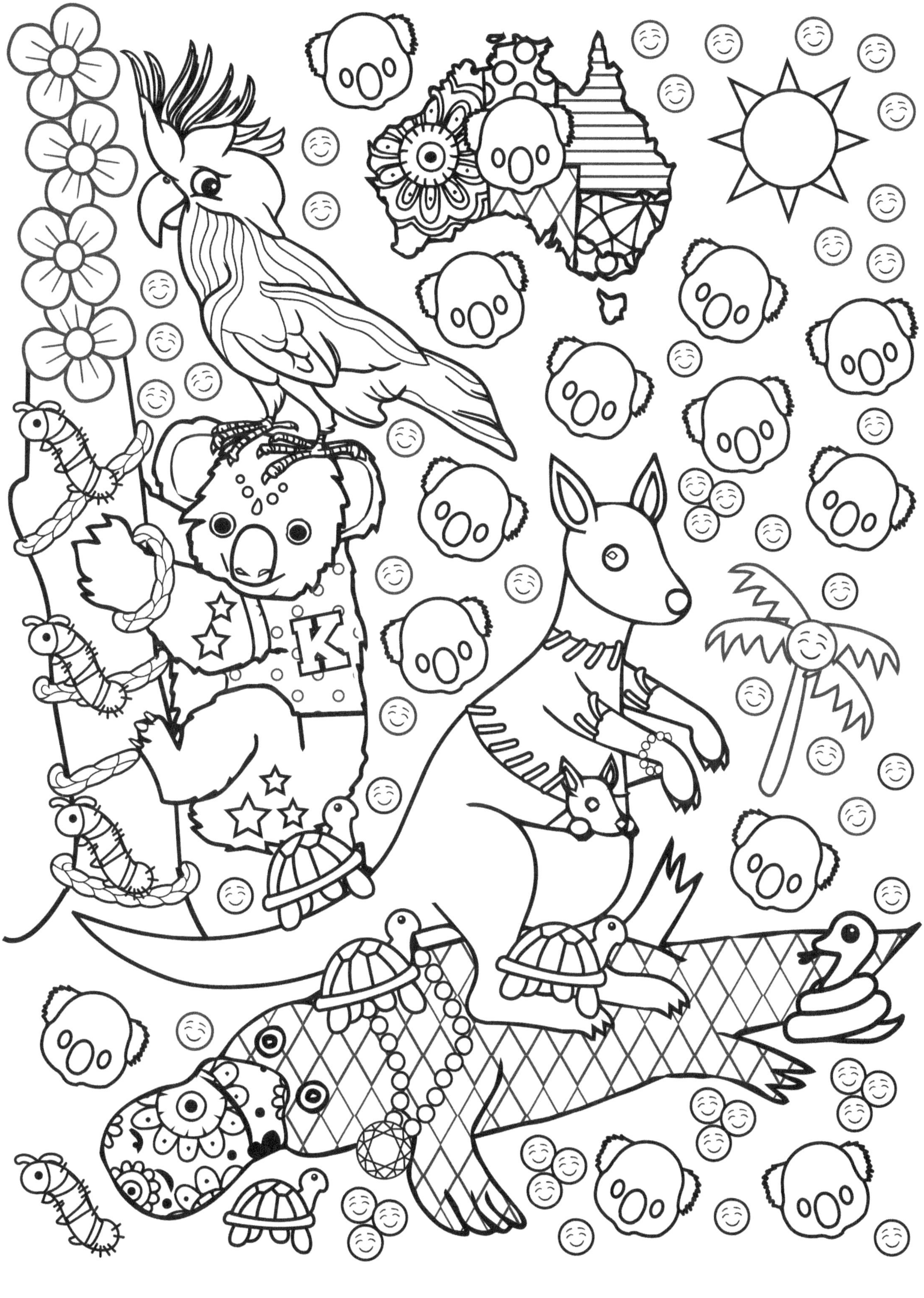
K

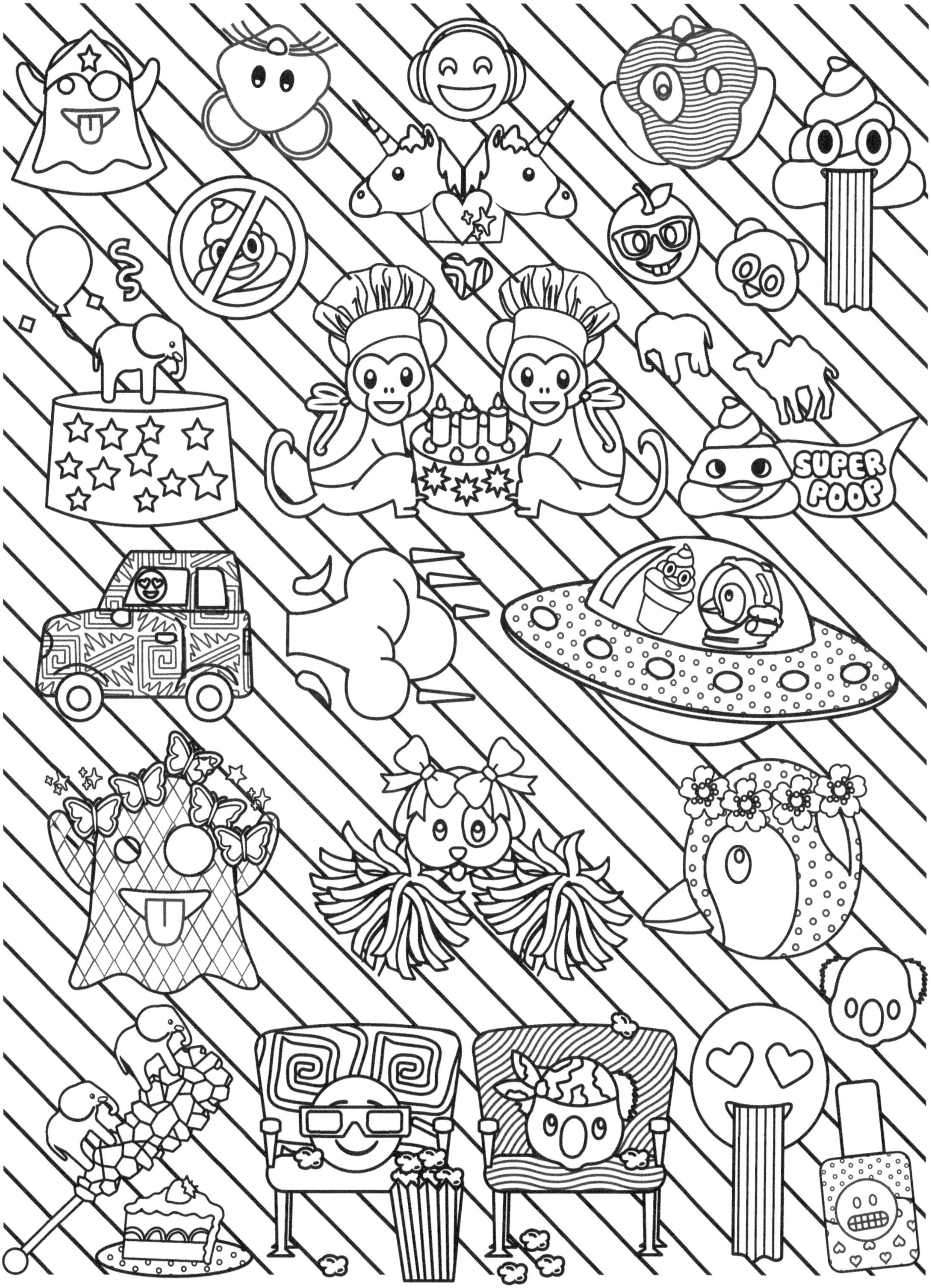
SUPER
POOP

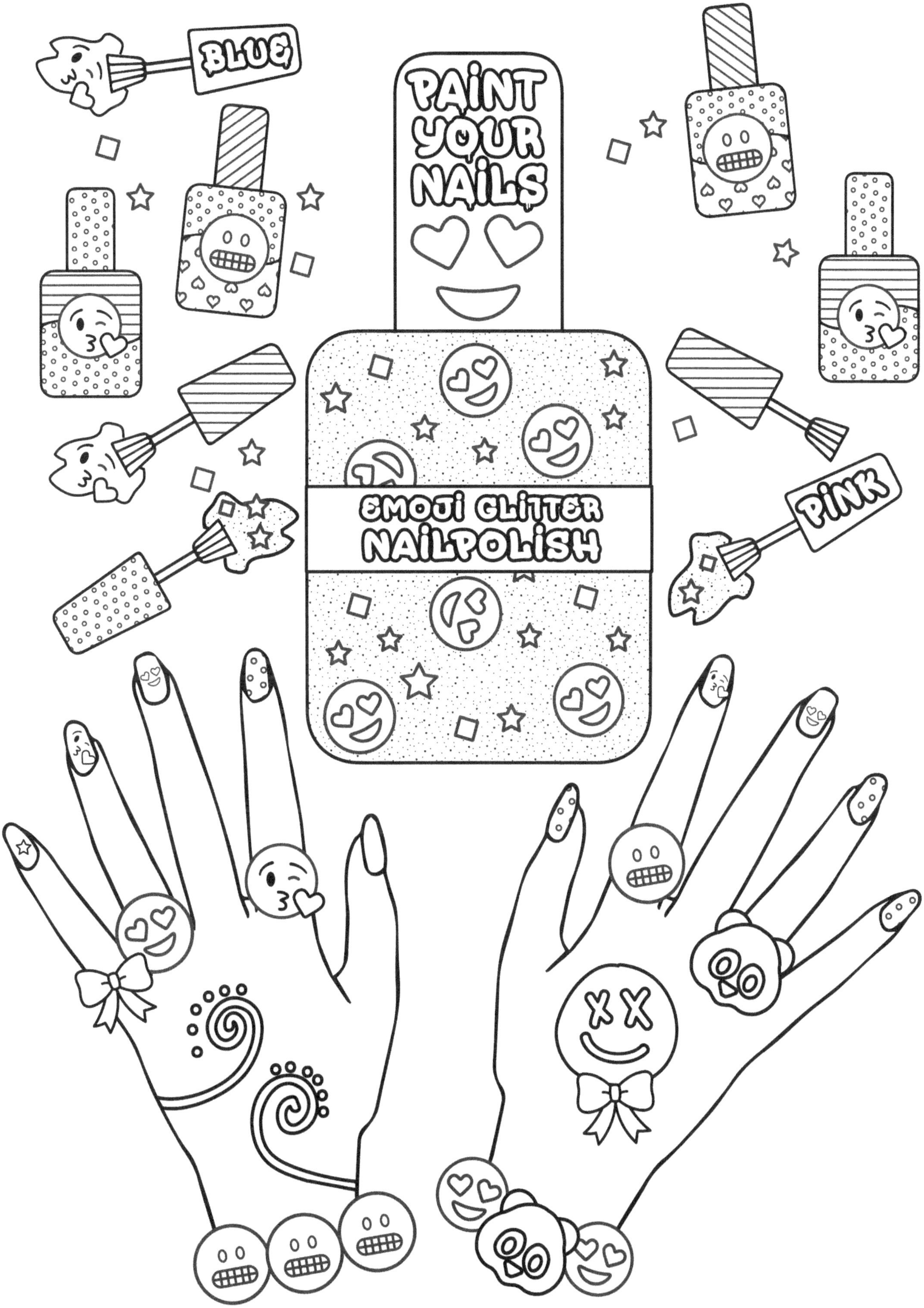
BLUE
PAINT YOUR NAILS
EMOJI GLITTER NAILPOLISH
PINK

www.ingramcontent.com/pod-product-compliance
Lightning Source LLC
Chambersburg PA
CBHW081308180526
45170CB00007B/2611
* 9 7 8 1 5 4 0 5 0 5 8 6 6 *